JEWELS
in a
CLAY POT

To: Semone
Fri: Donna
Be blessed

JEWELS
in a
CLAY POT
A depiction of life's journey

Donna Wilkinson Maxwell

XULON PRESS

Xulon Press
2301 Lucien Way #415
Maitland, FL 32751
407.339.4217
www.xulonpress.com

Xulon
PRESS

Paperback ISBN-13: 978-1-66286-255-7
Ebook ISBN-13: 978-1-66286-256-4

To my husband Peter, thank you for holding my hand through this journey of life. To my daughter Rene and grandchildren Roman and Morgan, my precious priceless jewels, you are forever in my heart. My parents Sydney and Doltry Wilkinson, I miss you beyond words. To my extended family and friends, thank you for being my muses.

Reverend Donna Maxwell has been able to capture the heart and passion of emotions that people express during the most difficult of circumstances, providing opportunities for reflection and healing as they travel through their most painful pathways. The words she expresses in her poems come forth with power and purpose. I endorse this compilation of life changing poems with great confidence that they will bring hope and comfort to many.

— *Bishop Dr. Jonathan Ramsey Jr.,*
author, Not Many Fathers

"A masterful collection of poems that could only have been divinely inspired. Filled with heart, love and understanding. It is as if Maxwell visited our lives, and delivered to us a heaven-filled perspective of our relationship with God and our purpose in His universe."

— *Gary Rhule, MD,*
author, Sailing on Broken Pieces.

Table of Contents

Hidden

I have,
Been through,
Some…stuff.
The "silver spoon" never touched the tip of my lips.
Scars, bruises and broken in some places,
Inquisitive glances show my lines and tear traces.
This path of life with its twists and turns
Has left me with some jagged edges and scabby road burns.
Though my exterior may seem weathered and hard,
It's the shield I carry as my guard
Yes, the shield I carry as my guard.

But,
There is…
A treasure I hide down on the inside;
Bountiful blessings in this broken weathered vessel
This clay pot marred and battered,
No external value but not to be discarded.
Its worth may not be readily seen
But remove the lid slowly and its treasures will be revealed.
Yes, remove the lid slowly…

Family

Where hearts are protected
No grudges stored or collected.
Surrounded by fierce defense
When confronted by external forces or offense.
The strongest relational bond on earth
Where endless love is brought forth.
Cocooned in the eternal love of our Father,
With no need to worry or fret about tomorrow.
A family who looks up to our God on high,
Full of mercy, grace and love, on Him we rely.
My family, yes that's us
Not ashamed of our faith, for in God we trust.
I pray your family will find the strength you need
To increase your faith in God,
Whose love you cannot supersede.
Go to God now for strength and power,
He'll be with you this very hour.

Speak Life

Sticks and stones may break my bones
But words cannot hurt me.
The innocent chanting of a child,
At insults being reeled overtly.

As we grew it became abundantly clear,
That once uttered they are in the atmosphere.
Words can form and transform us,
They can build us or destroy us.
The words you believe
Will dictate the life you will lead.

Today, I affirm you and speak life into your destiny
You are royal,
You are chosen,
Even when the contrary wind of life blows in.
You are the elect of God,
Called by God,
Special.
The Apple of God's eye;
These are the words I choose to leave for your life.
With your name written in the palm of His hand,
Hold your head up high as you stand.
Grounded by the life-giving Word
No longer afraid or stirred.
When the doubts arise and the fears dismay
And the words cut like a knife,
Your hope is assured and will not sway
For your name is written in the Lamb's Book of Life.

I Remember

When I am lonely, when I am blue
Lord, I'll always remember you.
The way you love me
The way you care
The way you adore me
You are ever near.
So, when I'm down hearted or in deep despair
I'll listen closely so I can hear
Your tender voice ever so dear.

Peace

Silent Assurance great confidence in God
That He will take care of all life's fears.
Silent assurance without saying a word
But trusting, believing your prayers are heard.
Silent assurance down on your knees,
God is able
He will do the deed.
Whatever your concern
Just be at peace
Silent assurance,
Thank God I am His.

Reflection

Cowering in the dark,
palms sweating.
All I can hear is the thumping beat of my heart.
Blood rushing, swishing in my head
What will happen?
Will I overcome or will I be dead...
How can I escape from this dread?
This terrible, morbid place of drear, doom and despair.
This darkness on the inside, tears flowing on the outside.
I slow my breathing...inhale, yes, exhale...deep
Do not think, do not even blink.
Just breathe, breathe, breathe...
Close my eyes to the world. To all those fears and
hurts and...
Not even sure what got me here in the first place.
What put me in this downward spiral of uncontrollable
gloom and despair?
STOP
Don't think, just breathe, breathe, breathe...
I open my eyes slowly, tomorrow is here!

I wake up from the terrible nightmare,
Inhale, exhale…breathe (repeat)
Another day has gone clear.

With this new day I stop to reflect,
What has caused this defect
in my life, my mind, my soul?
Why am I having these feelings of being less than whole?
Like Humpty Dumpty on the ground
Broken in pieces, some parts not found.
Was there something in my childhood,
Some abuse, neglect or insult of the intellect?
Was there something in my adolescence
It does not make much sense.
The one thing I do know,
I cannot return to that place of such anxiety and drear.
For I may not return when another day has gone clear.
So, what do I do to get by?
S T O P.
Don't think…
Just breathe…inhale, exhale, breathe…
Yes, another day has gone clear.

Terminal

Hustling, bustling going to and fro
Hustling, bustling I wonder where they go?
Purposefully wondering
I wonder what they're pondering
As they march in the direction
Of their planned destination.

As robot like automatons
Going around in circles in the queue,
Stay in line, be on time
As they tell you what to do.
Shoes, laptops, liquids in a bag
If they have to body search me,
I will most certainly gag!

Creeper

The cold steely hand of death sneaks into the
doorway of our lives
Death takes our loved ones and they are gone
He snatches the breath a little at a time
And we are all alone,
Alone to deal with the deep pain of loss
That hangs around our heart like an albatross.

Unbeknownst to us as to what he desires,
With his sinister plan and long black attire.
Dragging his gloomy tall, dark self,
knowing his plan full well as to where he will dwell.
He does not divulge whose breath he will take,
This is his secret, his plan to undertake.
So, here he comes down the hallway of our lives
To disrupt our rest for all times.
This is his job, he loves it well
As he makes his plans to cause us hell.
Will it be tragic or in our sleep?
The decision is made, his appointment to keep.
Try as we might, we cannot escape,
The cold steely hand of death is our fate.
His secret is deep and dark
He will not tell us until it's time to play our part.
It is a game of hide and go seek
I have sincere doubt that he is at his peak.

One by one he is taking our breath
This cold steely hand of death.

What is left when he has struck
But pain, despair and our lives just, "stuck"
Cannot feel, cannot move
Just a cloud of blurry haze
Heart hurt so deeply
Cannot function in the daze.
Will we ever feel the same again
As we plow through this mountain of pain?

But plow we must, that's our only way out
One day at a time, no doubt.
As time goes by the light gets brighter
We dig our way out and the pain gets lighter.
We hold our loved ones in our heart
Precious memories realized though we are apart.

So, when the steely hand of death
has marched down the corridor of your life,
Be strong and wait,
For the day is coming when you will appreciate
That your loved one is waiting at the gate.

Flickering star

I wish you had a chance at life,
For your childhood dreams were all so bright,
You loved to draw whatever you saw and had the
promise of innocence
raw.
You made your kites and watch them soar into the far beyond
Reaching the heights in life you would only dear to dream.
With secrets untold gleaming in your eyes,
songs composed by the soft
moonlight,
Strumming the keys of your guitar with visions
and glimmers under the
night's stars.
So, dream you did for hope was alive, you had
goals to reach, but time was
not on your side.
Your intellect would whisper its deepest
intentions as you'd pen new ideas
and witty inventions.

But opportunity was not to be the fulfillment of your destiny.
Innocence...gone
Songs...gone
Dreams...gone.
Flickered off into the night's sky
Your light in the distance, your passion, the crescendo of
your song.

Number 3

Proclamation!
Proclamation!
Emancipation Proclamation!
The freedom of a people, January first, 1863.
But, we were not all informed to the maximum degree;
Until General Order Number 3.
With General Order Number 3 in hand,
Major General Gordon Granger overcame the
resistance and took
a stand.
Free, free, you are free with absolute equality!
Was this true or was he speaking allegorically?
Equality of rights, rights for property this was read
to the Texas
nation,
Slaves went from shock and awe to jubilation.
June 19th, eighteen sixty-five
Was the date Texas slaves became alive.
Thirty months later than the entire country,
But better free, than not to be...
This sparked the Juneteenth Celebration,
Oldest national ending of slavery commemoration.
Juneteenth is a time for reflection and merriment,
To exercise the rights and privileges in the decree document.
A nation now groans under the pressure,
To find the life and equality that we all treasure.
The lives lost in the struggle, must never be forgotten,
All the dreams being born from the crop of the cotton.

Coalescence

How to bridge the great divide?
This question prevails from all sides.
A pebble dropped in the sea of life.
A ripple was started to eradicate the wrongs that pierced the
heart like a knife.
You humbled yourself to this daunting task,
To change a people and remove the mask.
To bridge the chasm of this great divide,
A task embarked upon as lives collide.
An obligatory hello to assuage the soul,
Conversations began one step at a time was the goal.
There are differences, this is true.
Does that make you better than me or me better than you?
The answer to the question will be revealed in time
Was your legacy embedded in these lives sublime?
We can only hope that as the conversations began
They won't fall by the wayside of the diversity plan.
Rest assured that the mark you've made
Will be with me for eternity as your kind words will not fade.
Words, spoken in a brief moment in time,
Unforgettable was the subject for it was symbolic of the
rhetoric of our lives.

Missing You

It was a Saturday morning just like this
My mom went home to The Lord to remain forever in
His bliss.
I know she was in pain and life was at its end
I had to let her go and watch her transcend.
Tears flowed like rain
For my mind could not comprehend
That I would never see her in this life ever again.
It's especially hard for me I say
On a Saturday morning like today
That deep ache just won't go away,
For it brings me back to that place
When I saw the last embers of youth
In my beautiful, adoring, loving mother's face.

Mom it was so hard for me to see you go...

Melody at dawn

I lay awake waiting for you in anticipation
Without you there is no life, no light
The trees lose their luster
The birds no longer sing their sweet melody
There is a quiet hush
Life is silent.
But as sure as the breath I breathe
I wait for you.
Your shadow is cast and my heart skips a beat.
I feel your warmth and life begins to stir.
The flowers bloom, the butterfly skips across the sky,
The morning glory unravels into full bloom.
You sustain me as you surround every part of my being.
My limbs stretch towards you, my star...my Helios.
Even in the obscurity of life, I just wait for you.
I know you are there.
So roll back dark clouds,
For I want to feel my light of day.
I am the apple of your eye.
Your glory is manifested in me.
My presence brings meaning and purpose to your existence.
Your energy is not wasted
For I am a reflection of your unfurling power,
Your reason to shine
Magnificence personified.

Wounded

Wounded by a nation that will not let us grow,
Questions unanswered and no reasons to show.
Suffering the atrocities from a country built on our back,
Beatings, maiming, hangings. Always under attack.
How can we get from under this laborious cash cow?
We demand justice and we want it now!
The deep seeded hate has taken root
With a license to kill…aim, trigger pulled…shoot.
Warriors deeply wounded but standing tall
Unsure of the future or the reason for our fall.
How will the wounds heal if you keep peeling back the scab?
The blood flows unboundedly as you continuously stab.
Backs bent low from the pressure and pain
The more I bend, the more you stomp, it's plain
I refuse to move as I have all to gain
Endure I must to be triumphant over this impenetrable
terror of reign.
Warriors deeply wounded but standing tall
Unsure of the future or the reason for our fall.
How can we contain or rationalize in our brain,
The magnitude of their disdain as crimson falls like rain?
Warrior, what is your war cry?
We need help and reinforcement. On each other we must rely.
So arch your back and wail if you must.
Defeat is not an option
For in God we trust.

As the pain becomes a dull ache
Through the veracity of our outcry
Statuesque we stand or we will die.
The stance of determination and unbending will
For generations fallen to the dust
Our promise to fulfill.
Hope unyielding in the struggle for equality
Freedom a must in its totality.
Irrevocable rights bestowed by the Creator
Life, liberty and happiness we demand it now, not later.
So, peel back the mask of indifference.
Pretense that there is no sufferance,
Will not nullify the fact that there is an unjustified
guilty sentence.
Warriors deeply wounded but standing tall
Unsure of the future or the reason for our fall.

Tribute to my Friend

Friends for life is what we'd say
Never dreamed we'd be separated today.
I think back to when our friendship began
It was second grade on FTPS land.
We had so much in common as we found out
Name, birth month gave us lots to talk about.
Never dreamed we'd be separated but that was our fate
To the United States I had to migrate.
We lost contact throughout the years,
The friend of my heart that I held dear
Life became complicated as it often does
But we knew it would all work out, just because.
In two thousand thirteen my circle was complete
The separation thing I did not want to repeat.
For a few good years we shared our families and lives.
We even reminisced on the years from the annals of
FTPS archives.
Yes, the friend of my heart was back to stay,
Until I got the message on that fateful Sunday.
Shattered, my heart on the floor,
Never dreamed we'd be separated again, I hurt to the core.
On the wings of the morning, she took her leave,
Family and friends could only grieve.
The legacy left behind of friendship, joy and hope
A life well lived with dignity, she somehow coped.
So, lift your eyes up to the sky,
Her spirit is free, no more tears to cry.
Her Mona Lisa smile will forever be
The trademark of her identity.

A Godmother's Prayer

Father, this gift of love bestowed on me
Is presented to you eternally.
Her life you've planned,
Her destiny in time written on the sand.
Plans for prosperity, hope and a future;
The Word of God her inspirational teacher.
Glory and honor her crown of splendor
The blessings of God I pray will always surround her.
Safely protected in Your loving care,
Always nestled in Your arms so dear.
Guarded by angels from above:
Goodness and mercy and always love.
Ethereal in nature, humility at its best,
Full of wisdom, a prophet as her name suggests.
Psalm 139 is hers to keep.
For you oh God neither slumber nor sleep.
You've watched over her before she was born
And protected her from life's thistles and thorns.
No matter where the journey of life meanders,
Your throne is accessible with fervor and candor.
So, into Your Hands I commend my Goddaughter
May her heart never fail and her steps never falter.
In Jesus' name I pray, amen.

Lady...Angel

Prim and proper, that's the lady we know
No pomp or circumstance, no... never for show
She glides as she walks;
Smiles as she talks;
Lady of intention and purpose
With depth of character,
Not superficial or on the surface.
She comes when you call,
Never says "no", not at all
Day or night, whatever the cause
She'll be at your doorstep without even a pause.
Humility is her name
But you can call her Lady all the same
For that's who she symbolizes...
Soft, gentle woman of character, wife, mother, sister, aunt...
And that's not even the end
But these are some of the words that describe my beautiful
sister friend.
Her ministry is service, her motive is love
To all she encounters, she's a gift from above.
Her generosity is unparalleled, unmatched by the masses,
Not to be superseded by gender or social classes.
She is on assignment, cocooned in earthly things.
We are all blessed to be brushed by the touch of her angel
wings.

Emerald Paradise

Forever I will hold you dear, Emerald Paradise –
Island so fair.
From up high I see your mountains jutting up into the sky.
Green and lush as if painted by brush.
Golden sand, azure sky and emerald sea.
Intoxicated by your beauty, my island fair.
O how I long, I long to be there.
As the iron bird swoops down and metal claws grip
the ground.
I feel the pulsing vibration of your beautiful sound
The call of the island as it surrounds me
I feel giddy as the music enfolds me
The beat of the drums, the depth of the base
The rhythm so strong, I cannot escape.
Natural as the air I breathe my body sways to the jewel
under my feet.
The beat of the island seeping in my bones
A love I feel deep down in my soul.
A part of me, I cannot deny.
A pride that goes deeper, not hard to identify.
It is greater than me, a pride in my heritage: a long history
of independence; of
non-conformists that produced our heroes, a nation of
enduring people who will go down in infamy.
No matter where I go, all roads must lead home to the
Emerald Paradise of my heart: sweet, sweet Jamaica.

Haiti's Bleeding Soul

The soul of Haiti crying out,
Hands lifted high, sighing out
From the dust and dirt, dying out.

Father, your people need your help
Their needs are showing out
The faces waiting now
For your love to reveal its hidden glow;
But the dark clouds hover and they hang low.

Rain, Lord, on my Haitian brothers and sisters
Rain your crimson love
For the rainbow will burst through like hope
Fulfilling your promise from above.

The soul of Haiti will breathe again
Like dry bones from the dust and pain, again
Not forgotten by your mighty hand,
The soul of Haiti will always stand.

Our lives are changed forever Lord
By the sights imprinted in our hearts.
Never to be forgotten but impressed to do more,
For your service and your presence Lord.
In surrender, we open our hearts and hands;
For your blood was shed for this land.

Ode to a Stranger

Strange country, strange land, strange people.
A child lost and alone in a world of my own
I was far, far away from the place I called home
Wandering the streets of the town.
"This is the last stop," that's what the driver said.
"Get off the bus for the trip is at its end."
So, there I stood lost in this strange land,
As innocent as could be, I asked a random stranger if he
would help me,
Not knowing what else to do.
The sun was hanging low and the wiles of the concrete
jungle were too.
The memory of this stranger's kindness indelibly imprinted
in my brain,
His kindness he extended to me, he had nothing to gain.
For he walked me home through that dangerous zone,
He made sure the little lost girl got safely home.
The last dollar in my pocket I offered to him.
He would not take it for his kindness was from within.
Deep within the recesses of this stranger's heart,
His care and concern for me could not be bought.
I recant this story for it warms my heart so,
The kindness of that stranger so long, long ago.
I think of him often and wish I could repay,
The nameless, faceless stranger of that cold September day.

Church Angels

You have been anointed and appointed by God's
Almighty Hand.
Your lives dedicated to His Providence and His plan.
Destined to lead the people of God,
The Commission was given as He directs the path you
must trod.
Ministers of the Gospel, teach and preach,
Preach to the lost and undone.
Preach Pastors, preach for at the end there'll be no place for
them to run.
Let the Word of God go forth on the airwaves,
To conquer the sin that enslaves.
Preach pastors, preach for generations to come are
depending on your persistence.
To impact lives in anticipation of their existence.
Preach the good tidings,
Bind up the broken hearts,
Preach of the coming of the Lord,
For hell is the destination if not on God's accord.
Preach pastors, preach.
Preach of the good news, the message of peace and hope,
For life gets difficult and it's hard to cope.
Share the Word of eternal life,
In this world riddled with sin and strife.
Preach of the Blood of Jesus and His cleansing power
That grants deliverance any time, any hour.

Preach of the God who reigns forever.
He is coming back again, our Lord and Savior,
The Lord of Hosts is His name,
Faithful and True, one in the same.
Preach of the marriage supper of the Lamb.
We will be clothed in fine linen,
As in His presence we stand.
Priests of the Lord, Ministers of our God,
The riches of the wicked belongs to you; the just.
God has promised you double for your trouble when in Him
you trust.

Frosty Night

Moonbeams on the snow-covered ground bathe the night's
sky with their silvery glow.
Crisp and clear the dense cold night air hangs and penetrates
the whole atmosphere.
The snow, like frozen cotton balls dangle from
tentacled limbs
Reaching, reaching high,
Nearly touching the luminescent winter sky.
Shadowy figures in the night gives way to visions in the
subtilty of the conscious mind.

Abide with me

Forever a constant guide for me,
A humble follower I will be.
Precious Lord, abide with me.
Your crimson blood was shed,
As you hung your head and said,
"It is finished."
The price has been paid,
For me to be Your earthly aide.
You'll carry my prayers on angel's wings
And bottle my tears so I can sing.

Silent Scream

Young brother gone too soon,
Cut down in your prime,
Well before your time.
And, some had the audacity to say,
"it's not a crime."

Young brother gone too soon,
Your legacy cut down.
You were made level to the ground.
Was anyone else around?
Did someone hear a sound?
Or did they hide
behind their suburban blind?

Young brother: innocent, innocent, innocent.
I shake my head and cry in despair.
I still hear past generations crying in fear.
INNOCENT.
INNOCENT.
INNOCENT.
Will anyone ever give a care?

Frivolity

Laa, la, laa,
Laa, la, laa.
Running through the lily fields,
Skipping head over heels.
Smiling at the sun with elation,
Butterfly floats by,
What a creation!

Not a care in the world,
Not a thought in my brain.
I'm enjoying this moment,
And feeling no pain.
I laugh out loud from deep inside,
That thought was so crazy,
It overwhelmed me like a tide.

Going with the flow,
No place to go.
I'm just being,
Don't care if I'm seen
Just enjoying this moment of sheer indulgence.
O my, this absolutely makes no sense.

Man of Valor

Tried and true, that's what we say about you.
A man among men, one of a few.
Reliable, dependable always accessible to lend a helping hand,
Even when the work is not popular or grand.
Calm, sincere showing just how much you care,
By always, always being there.

You are appreciated for all that you do;
A pure heart of gold, it's true.
For cutting our lawn, shoveling our snow.
You care for us, even when on the go.
Calling and visiting no matter the time,
Even falling asleep at the drop of a dime.

Thank you for the man you are:
A man of valor, our north star.
The English language is not sufficient,
So, we circled the globe to be proficient.
Here are the languages to show our gratitude,
For a man of your stature and great fortidude:

Swazi and Zulu	Ngiyobonga
Swahili	Asante
Spanish	muchas gracias
Scots	Thank ye, ta
Portugese	Obrigato
Japanese	Arigatogozaimasu
French	Merci beaucoup
Dutch	Dank U
Afrikaans	Dankie

The Great Mystery

Before the foundation of the world, the hidden mystery
was wrought.
Through the wisdom of God, the plan in place our salvation
was bought.
For His predestined, His royal priesthood, His chosen
from above,
Holy and blameless covered by the blood of love.
The mystery was hidden from the princes of this world, they
didn't know the
Lord of glory nor the plan to be unfurled.
They didn't know Him in the garden as He prayed, His tears
became as drops
of blood His life betrayed.
They didn't know the King of glory as they placed the crown
of thrones on
His brow.
They scourged His back and thought, "we will
silence Him now…"
They didn't know the King of glory as they led Him
up the hill
to the death of the cross so He'd be still.
The mystery was hidden as they nailed His hands and feet.
"It is finished," He said.
They thought He cried in defeat.
Then He hung His head…dead.
Dead, they pronounced Him dead.
In a tomb they placed Him in a rich man's stead.

Behind a tomb of rocks and stone, the King of glory laid,
all alone.
This was not the end for the Lord of Glory would transcend.
On the third day, He rose again revealing the mystery since
time began.
The secret exposed for all to see, the King of glory rose
in victory,
Triumphing over the enemy.
Lost and undone we've been reconciled by the Son.
Before the foundation of the world, the hidden mystery
was wrought.
Through the wisdom of God, the plan in place our salvation
was bought.
God manifested in the flesh, justified in the Spirit, seen of
angels, preached
unto the Gentiles, believed by the world, received up
into glory,
And that is just the beginning of the story.
If the princes of this world knew the Lord of glory, they
would not have
crucified Him.

The Joy of Christmas

The joy of Christmas is not in the presents neatly wrapped,
Or even sitting on Santa's lap.
It's not in the trees as they glisten and glow,
With the first sprinkles of snow.
It's not the hustle and bustle of shopping at the mall,
No, that's not it at all.
It's not even the excitement of a child
Waiting to open their gifts on Christmas morn.
This is NOT why Jesus was born.

The joy of Christmas humbly born in a manger.
Heralded by angels.
Honored by kings.
He came to us on a quiet night,
With deliverance in His wings.

The joy of Christmas grew with care.
The traditions of His Father, He held dear.
At twelve years old He sat in the temple,
Conversing with doctors
Who were astonished at His example.
His Father's business was His goal,
As He sat in the synagogue and read the scroll.

The joy of Christmas had a mission.
His Father's plan seen to completion.
He knew the road He had to trod,
Even in the garden when His tears
Flowed liked drops of blood.

Ten thousand angels He could have called.
But who would bring deliverance to us all?
The joy of Christmas had to die.
Our redemption He paid
As the blood flowed from His side.
Darkness came down,
The temple's foundation torn,
For this, the joy of Christmas was born.

But He could not be held by the cold hands of death.
On the third day He burst the tomb.
He defied the laws of our reality
To fulfil His destiny.
The joy of Christmas that's who He is,
The Son of God, He lives.

As He sits in splendor on the right hand of power,
We bring our gifts to Him.
Not as the wisemen with gold, frankincense or even myrrh,
But we give Him praise with humble hearts true.
Living sacrifices, one and all,
Contrite and broken to the Spirit's call.
Wonderful, Counsellor, Mighty God,
Everlasting Father, the Prince of Peace,
The King whose star was seen in the East.

Joy of Christmas, Jesus is His name.
The reason for the season,
We are glad He came.
With elation and jubilee, we herald His glory.
With hands held high we celebrate His story.

Listening Ear

What do you hear, listening ear,
As lives are poured out to you?
Not holding anything back…
Personal, intimate and deep.
Can't move, can't stir, can't even make a peep.

Just be there listening ear, for this is what is needed.
Take it in, pass it on to the heart,
So a response can be clear and unimpeded.

The heart ponders, considers all that comes in,
Muses on a response to the woe.
A heart true blue that will not disappoint,
But will be there in whatever you undergo.

In silence, I ponder, I muse and I wonder.
What will the heart say to that?
For it's a problem so deep,
The ear cannot keep,
But the heart knows just where it's at.

Adolescence

Girl growing up,
Changing, re-arranging;
Not sure what to do,
Who to see,
Where to be,
Complicated…that's me.

Trying to figure it out,
What this life's all about.
I am quiet, I look inside,
When I really just wanna shout.
Complicated…yes, that's me.

Not as simple as it seems,
Matured beyond my age.
Watching, observing,
Taking it all in.
Not wanting to go through YOUR pain.
Yes, complicated, me.

When I seem to be melancholy,
As some young ladies are,
It's just that I'm deep inside,
Insecure, unsure by far.
Just remind me of the princess that I am,
The promise of life instore.
Help me to get over myself,
As my journey just began,
This life to explore.
Complicated, for sure.

Close the Door

My love, let us close the door to the world
So that we can be alone together
As we gaze into each other's heart.
The rhythm of our lives beating to that familiar sound
For we are bone of our bones,
Flesh of our flesh. We are one.

Let us close the door to the world
As we live the vow: To have and to hold
My love from this day into eternity.
Let us languish here awhile,
Loving, cherishing
The rhythm of our lives beating to that familiar sound.
As I gaze upon my love, I see the reflection:
One body, one heart, one flesh.

Come away with me my love,
Close the door of the world.
As we are lost in each other's heart,
We soar as eagles with the love we share.
Let's languish here for awhile,
For we exist only for each other.

Love Morphs

When our love was young,
You gazed into my eyes,
Held my hand on our strolls,
Opened the door.
I could do no wrong.
You protected me
And made me feel safe.
You kissed me with such passion,
My knees were weak
And my heart skipped a beat.
Your arms embraced me and
Nothing else mattered.
You admired my walk,
The sound of my voice.
You had eyes only for me.
We were together every day,
Together.

As our love matured,
We would talk for hours about our day,
what life has in store,
And how we would rock in our chairs on the porch
In our later years,
Together.

We would laugh and sometimes cry,
Talking about the years gone by.
Now settled in our love,
Some things may have changed over the years.
The walk may be different,
Knees a little weaker.
There may be things that we've done wrong but,
Baby, you still excite me.

Your laughter is like water over the waterfalls,
That familiar rumble from deep within.
You still make me feel like it's Christmas,
Over, and over and over again.
I feel loved.
Protected.
Safe.
Although our love has changed,
It remains the same,
For we are
Together.

Armored Knight

Tall, dark and handsome may be overrated.
A good man comes in all sizes and shades.
Six figures or seven may be over stated,
As the size of his income does not a man make.
A man to take charge is what you are seeking?
But if he takes charge of you,
You may be fleeing.

What does a lady really want?
A gentleman all the time, not only in her prime.
No matter the color of his skin,
As long as he lets Jesus in.
To hold her in his loving arms
As they travail through life and its sudden alarms.
Walking together down the road of life,
Not be a slave for him in the disguise of a wife.
Discard the rose-colored glasses
For the glitter you see will fade
With life's circumstances.

When Water Speaks

How does one verbalize or articulate
The character of a man
Who does not generate much conversation or debate?
How can one put into words his opinion
When they are hardly ever heard?
He personifies the colloquialism,
"Silent river runs deep."
Whose waters flow smooth and still
With no evidence of the rocks beneath.
The trials of life with edges sharp,
Some smooth and slippery
In waters dark.
Do not be confused by the meek exterior
Or attempt to exploit what you think to be inferior.
A bridled stallion for sure,
Choosing to submit to the God he adores.
Make no mistake of this power under constraint
As he labors continuously without a word of complaint.
Hold your head high, humble servant.
Let the quiet waters flow,
For what God has promised you, He will bestow.

Flowers in the Wind

I recall the day you left,
With bated breath, I deeply wept.
Broken hearted deep inside,
No one to quelch the overwhelming tide.
On that fated day in June,
I felt you'd left me way too soon.

I tried to hold on and pleaded for you not to leave.
In desperation and despair, I tried to cleave.
You wet your lips to quench the thirst.
The tears ran down my face as my heart burst.
Staring off into the distance,
Being beckoned into the unknown.
You left me in an instance
And I was all
Alone.

But it's your birthday today
And I brought you some flowers
Bathed in my tears for the last few hours.
You've been in this spot laying under this tree.
The gentle breeze blowing,
You were set free.

I share my secrets as you lay still
In this shady glen on the top of this hill.
I carry you in the broken pieces of my heart,
For I know we are never apart.
I lay the flowers down that were watered with care.
I will miss your presence always,
My darling mother dear.

I wait

With heavy eyes I take my rest,
Drifting off into sweet serenity.
My thoughts are filled with you.
Two strangers yearning for each other,
Soulmates lost in the haze of time.
I know you are there.
I succumb to the pleasurable respite of sleep,
Where I can languish in the essence of you.
Strangers, but I dream of the day
When you become my reality.
An emotional state of euphoria,
Heart beating in my chest,
Can't breathe.
Intoxicated with the scent of you.
I dream of you, my love.
We hold hands tightly,
As we walk by the light of the moon.

As we meet
Not a moment goes by
Without my thoughts being filled with you.
Our lives and private moments
With secret smiles shared by two.

I pray this moment never ends,
For you are my sphere,
My world.
Hearts beating as one,
Bodies held tightly.
Shadows cast to the ground,
As we saunter by the light of the moon.

I dream and patiently wait for you,
My perfect stranger.
We will know when our reality blooms
And will recognize each other's heart.
Until then my love,
I open my arms and my heart
And I wait only for you.

Circle

They hold you close and encircle you,
The feeling of a cozy fire, soft blanket.
You feel warm.
There is no sense of danger or harm.
These arms protect you from the world and all its misery.
The arms of a mother, what a mystery.
Arms so dear,
None can compare
To the love that they give.
When they can no longer hold you
And are weak and feeble,
Can they count on you?
Cozy fire?
Soft blanket?
Protection from lurking danger?

Sleep

So elusive at times,
Yet I yearn for it.
Essential to life,
My eyes burn for it.
Body breaks down,
I can't turn to it.

Oblivion

Living in Oblivion,
At ease on the side lines of ignorance.
The world goes by, not begging for deliverance.
There's this utopia in my head,
In reality I refuse to tread,
As I blissfully wallow in my shallow existence.

Hope

Hope stands alone,
Ever looking upwards
With a joyful heart.
Expressions of praise are echoed,
Requests are made known to God.
Hands lifted high to heaven,
Hearts overflow with praise.
Looking always upwards,
Never ending Hope.

The Plan

Among the olive trees He bowed His head,
His sweat became as drops of blood, they said.
Exceedingly sorrowful in agony, He prayed,
While His inner circle...stayed.

In the Garden of Gethsemane among the olive plants,
The crushing and pressing were not by chance.
His flesh had to submit to what the Spirit had to accomplish.
His plan to fulfil, our sins to abolish,
Constrained by the Father's will.
Not far away the inner circle slept...still.
Not even for an hour could you watch and pray,
Eyes wide open, temptation at bay?
No further response did He seek,
For the spirit was willing but the flesh was weak.
In the garden He came to terms,
While the angel ministered strength, the plan affirmed.
Resolute He stood,
As the enemy came upon Him, as he should.
There in the garden, the Lord was apprehended,
The Plan set in motion as God had intended.

CPSIA information can be obtained
at www.ICGtesting.com
Printed in the USA
JSHW060512301122
34024JS00002B/5

9 781662 862557